TEACHER'S TOOLS - COMPREHENSION QUESTIONS ON... GOODNIGHT MISTER TOM

Róisín Beaver

Copyright © 2023 Róisín Beaver

All rights reserved

The characters and events portrayed in this book are fictitious. Any similarity to real persons, living or dead, is coincidental and not intended by the author.

No part of this book may be reproduced, or stored in a retrieval system, or transmitted in any form or by any means, electronic, mechanical, photocopying, recording, or otherwise, without express written permission of the publisher.

Cover design by: Art Painter
Library of Congress Control Number: 2018675309
Printed in the United States of America

To hardworking teachers everywhere

CONTENTS

Title Page
Copyright
Dedication
Goodnight Mister Tom   1
Chapter One   2
Chapter Two   4
Chapter Three   5
Chapter Four   6
Chapter Five   7
Chapter Six   8
Chapter Seven   9
Chapter Eight   10
Chapter Nine   11
Chapter 10   12
Chapter 11   13
Chapter 12   14
Chapter 13   15
Chapter 14   16
Chapter 15   17
Chapter 16   18
Chapter 17   19

Chapter 18	20
Chapter 19	21
Chapter 20	22
Chapter 21	23
Chapter 22	24
Chapter 23	25

GOODNIGHT MISTER TOM

By Michelle Magorian

CHAPTER ONE

1. Who did Tom see when he opened his door?
2. Describe Tom Oakley.
3. What was the first thing Tom asked Willie to do to make him feel at home?
4. Briefly describe the front room.
5. How did Willie feel as he sat on the stool by the fire?
6. What did Tom notice about Willie's legs?
7. Willie's mum said she was kinder to him than most mothers – how?
8. When Willie looked out into the garden he felt something was missing – what was it?
9. What kind of teacher was Mr. Barrett?
10. What did Willie see scrabbling in the leaves and how did he feel initially?
11. What had Willie's mother told him about dogs?
12. When Tom found Willie threatening his dog Willie thought he was going to do something to him – what was it?
13. Tom had heard stories about evacuees – what were they supposed to be like? How was Willie different?
14. Tom tells Sammy that he doesn't know much about children, but he does know not to treat them a certain way – what does he say?
15. Why was the ladder to the attic not used in forty years?
16. What did Tom keep of Rachel's belongings?
17. What had happened to Tom's baby son?

Vocabulary

1. imminent 2. abruptly 3. subsided 4. clad 5. alcove
6. poisonous
7. obligatory 8. intently 9. reverberated 10. adamant
11. venomous
12. robust 13. unperturbed

CHAPTER TWO

1. How does Willie know Sammy likes him?
2. Willie notices something unusual about the cottages – what was it?
3. What does Tom ask Mrs. Fletcher to do?
4. How do we know Tom is a rather abrupt person?
5. At the farm Willie sees something he has never seen before – what was it?
6. What does Tom tell Ivor?
7. Describe Lucy.
8. What are the blackouts for?
9. Name the village.
10. What has Mrs. Beech put in Willie's bag for "when he's bad"?
11. What did Mrs. Beech mean by "I've sewn him in for the winter"?
12. How did Tom make Willie pyjamas?
13. Tom handed Willie some cake – what was Willie thinking?
14. Describe Willie's room
15. What was unusual about Willie's reaction to the bed?
16. What was Tom muttering to himself that evening? What does it tell us about Tom?

Vocabulary

1. scudded   2. ecstatically   3. incoherently   4. gruff   5. bewildering
6. torrent   7. flinched   8. rapt

CHAPTER THREE

1. What had woken Willie up?
2. What had he done when he was asleep?
3. What did Willie keep saying to Tom?
4. What did Tom find out about Willie when he left him to write a postcard?
5. When was Willie born?
6. Who got to paint when Willie was at school?
7. Why was Willie so surprised when Tom said 'Good' to him?
8. Why did Tom visit Doctor Little?
9. What did the doctor suggest to help Willie?
10. Mrs. Little gave Tom something to help heal Willie's sores – what was it?
11. What did Mrs. Little give Willie for his socks and why was he so happy?
12. What was the trench in the Little's garden for?
13. What was the boy in the post office doing that caught Willie's attention?
14. Charles Ruddles gave out to Tom – why?

Vocabulary

1. retch   2. voluminous   3. impotently   4. resumed   5. pursue
6. malnutrition   7. garter   8. deteriorated   9. spasm
10. wryly   11. endowed   12. declared

CHAPTER FOUR

1. Why was Willie having difficulty in the sweet shop?
2. Describe the evacuated children
3. What cloth did Willie like at the drapers and why?
4. What shop did Willie want to look into?
5. They go into the library, what does Willie ask Tom about?
6. Why was Willie so anxious when he asked Tom for help in the library? What did Willie want Tom to help him with?
7. What does Tom tell Willie when Willie asks if he was angry with him?

Vocabulary

1. equipped   2. jolted   3. horde   4. huskily   5. irritation   6. rigid
7. drapers   8. corduroy   9. craned   10. stifling   11. disarray
12. ominously   13. irritable   14. suppressed   15. unceasingly
16. exploits

CHAPTER FIVE

1. Name the teachers in the school
2. What did Tom say they had to do that afternoon?
3. Did Willie like his new boots?
4. Why was Willie bewildered when the vicar asked him to put out the bibles?
5. Why did Willie dread the Sunday service?
6. Willie was shocked by Nancy Little – why?
7. What was the surprise for Willie's birthday?
8. What was Tom's advice when the congregation were singing hymns?
9. Name the Prime Minister
10. Why were people upset at what the Prime Minister had to say?
11. What were the evil things named by the Prime Minister?
12. What were Sunday's for according to Willie's mother?
13. What was it that Willie didn't know how to do?
14. What did the choirboy ask Mr. Tom for?
15. Why was Sammy miserable?

Vocabulary

1. panorama   2. reveries   3. permeated   4. assortment   5. spellbound
6. obstruction   7. riveted   8. oppression   9. persecution   10. prevail
11. interminable   12. involuntary   13. malice   14. scrutinizing
15. reticent   16. fervour   17. silhouetted

CHAPTER SIX

1. Why did Willie almost drop the clod of earth he was holding?
2. Where were the First Aid Post and Rest Centre to be located?
3. What did Tom volunteer for?
4. Tom also volunteered the services of Dobbs and the cart – why?
5. Why does Zach call Willie 'Will'?
6. Why was Willie so scared of the large copper tub?

Vocabulary

1. penetrate   2. recluse   3. exuberant   4. anticipated   5. precariously
6. inconspicuously   7. cultured   8. partake   9. voluble
10. interspersed
11. sagacity

CHAPTER SEVEN

1. Why did Willie think he was a sissie after all?
2. What was Tom's advice?
3. What did George ask Tom?
4. What did George think about 'townees'?
5. What had Willie and Zach brought with them?
6. What had Mrs. Little threatened Zach with?
7. What does 'Delumptious' mean according to Zach?
8. Why had Willie's mum told him to make himself invisible?
9. Why did Willie panic when asked what he liked?
10. What did a swallow mean to Willie?
11. What had Tom done to the shelter?
12. What did Willie think about that night as he fell asleep?

Vocabulary

1. nonchalantly 2. interposed 3. glutinous 4. incoherently
5. reputation 6. consumed

CHAPTER EIGHT

1. George was happy to see such a crowd at school – what did he say?
2. How old was Zach?
3. What did Willie do when he said he couldn't read or write?
4. How did Willie feel when he moved into Mrs Black's class?
5. Tom reckoned most of Mrs Black's time would be taken up with discipline. What did Tom offer to do to help Willie?
6. Why did Willie think about copying and what did Tom say?
7. What did George say to Willie about reading and writing?
8. Why did Charlie Ruddles stride angrily into Tom's house?

Vocabulary

1. dilapidated 2. anguish   3. dejected   4. frantically   5. aghast

CHAPTER NINE

1. What had the Padfields sent Willie?
2. What clothes did Willie receive as a present?
3. What did Emilia Thorne give Willie as a present and what was written on it?
4. What was the extra special present Tom gave Willie?
5. How did Willie feel inside the church when he first went in?
6. What was unusual about the cottage as Willie approached it?
7. What had Willie drawn?

Vocabulary

1. overcome   2. voluminous

CHAPTER 10

1. Why had some parents asked their children to return home to the cities?
2. How did Emilia Thorne help Willie to learn words?
3. What had Willie's mum said about theatres and cinemas?
4. Why wasn't there any description in a play according to Zach?
5. What did Willie learn about his name?
6. Why did Mrs Little interrupt them?
7. Describe Spooky Cott.
8. What idea did the children have for passing their time?
9. What had Zach said about Willie as a friend?
10. Why had Tom stuck labels in various places?
11. How does Tom show understanding when Willie asks to have his friends up in his room?

Vocabulary

1. despondently 2 emanating 3. unison

CHAPTER 11

1. Tom doesn't mind that Willie's mother isn't coming to visit – why is this?
2. How had Willie's room changed?
3. Why is Carrie so annoyed about boys?
4. What was unusual at the end of the chapter?

Vocabulary

1. unanimously 2. squat

CHAPTER 12

1. Tom shows his community spirit – how?
2. What had been happening outside Little Weirwold?
3. How did the events of war effect Emilia Thorne's job?
4. What were the children doing in the three weeks til Christmas?
5. How did Willie get himself into character?
6. What did Miss Thorne say about Zach and acting?
7. Why didn't Willie understand Zach when he told him he was a 'good actor'?
8. Why was Miss Thorne in such a bad humour when she came back in?
9. Why did Tom look so pale when Willie came home?
10. What had happened to Rachel?

Vocabulary

1. escalate 2. salvage 3. monotonously 4. intermittently 5. prompt 6. mesmerised 7. quota

CHAPTER 13

1. Willie has got to know Mister Tom very well; this is shown when Willie gets to Carol practice. What does Willie realise when he sees Tom?
2. Willie puts his imagination to good use when singing – what does he do?
3. Tom opens up to Willie again after Carol practice – how?

Vocabulary

1. brusquely 2. dirge 3 rendition 4. rousing 5. jaunty 6 crescendo

CHAPTER 14

1. Why was George wearing a black armband?
2. What was Carrie asking Mrs Hartridge?
3. What did Willie say, 'Everything takes its own time'?
4. What had Mrs Hartridge to say about Carrie?
5. Why did Patsy stare at Willie?
6. Painting had an effect on Willie – describe.
7. Describe Willie's painting.
8. How do you know Carrie is bright?
9. What objection did Carrie's mother have?
10. What was contained in the letter Tom received?

Vocabulary

1. exhilarated 2. surreptitiously 3. excelled 4. oblivious 5. scholarship 6. cadence

CHAPTER 15

1. How did Tom show his unwillingness to let Willie go?
2. Why did Tom advise Willie not to expect much from his mother?
3. Where did the soldier think Willie's dad was?
4. Why didn't Willie's mum recognise him?
5. Describe Mrs Beech.
6. Why did she feel threatened by Willie's smile?
7. How had the people of Little Weirwold shown their concern for Mrs Beech?
8. Why didn't Mrs Beech reply to Willie's letters?
9. How does Mrs Beech show she is two-faced?
10. What surprise does Willie get and how does he react?
11. How did Mrs Beech react to news of Willie's friend Zach?
12. Describe Willie when he woke.

Vocabulary

1. dejected 2. contemplate 3. multitude 4. significant 5. subservient 6. lenient 7. debauched. 8. scrutiny 9. blasphemy 10. congeal

CHAPTER 16

1. What did Mister Tom miss about Willie?
2. Mister Tom thought the reason Willie hadn't written was because......Complete this sentence.
3. Describe how Mister Tom stands out from the crowds when he reaches London.
4. Why was the warden puzzled at why Mister Tom has come to London?
5. How does the warden describe Willie and his mother?
6. How does Sammy help?
7. Describe what happens when they break in to the house.

Vocabulary

1. intermittent 2. dilapidated 3. tenements 4. brusque

CHAPTER 17

1. In your own words describe what was under the stairs.
2. Why did the warden allow Tom to continue?
3. Describe Trudy.
4. How did Tom explain the pains in Willie's arm?
5. What did Willie say happened when he got nightmares?
6. Why does Mr. Stelton want Will to go with him?
7. Was Mister Tom and Will's journey home an easy one? Why?
8. What had Dr. Little to say?

Vocabulary

1. alcove 2. emaciated 3. disperse 4. laboriously 5. manoeuvred 6. lacerations 7. delousing 8. bespectacled 9. sedate 10. regulations 11. furtive 12. contagious 13. expostulated 14. inert

CHAPTER 18

1. What did Rachel mean by telling Tom he'd have to get blue?
2. Why do you think Will got upset at hearing about Mrs Hartridge's baby girl?
3. Where does Will think babies come from?
4. What does Mister Tom reckon is wrong with Mrs Beech?
5. What did Mrs Hartridge do when there was a knock at the door? Why?

Vocabulary

1. hypodermic 2. pallid 3. rejuvenated 4. inconspicuously 5. despondently 6. elocution 7. prodigies 8. smote 9. avert 10. mesmerized

CHAPTER 19

1. Why had they left Dobbs with a farmer?
2. Why was Mrs Clarence delighted to have them to stay?
3. What effect did the sea have on Will?
4. How did Mrs Clarence's differ from Mister Tom's house?
5. What did Zach name the village?
6. Describe Mrs. Clarence's attitude towards Tom.
7. How did Zach and Will differ when swimming?
8. Why was Zach so worried at the news?
9. How had their holiday changed Zach and Will?

Vocabulary

1. azure 2. panniers 3. conspicuous 4. tandem 5. clambered 6. immerse 7. expanse 8. anticipation 9. emanated 10. populated 11. ravenous 12. incision 13. incessant 14. gorse 15. treading water 16. mournfully 17. mollycoddle 18. guttural 19. transfused 20. disarray

CHAPTER 20

1. Who did they meet in Spooky Cott?
2. How was he 'different'?
3. Why didn't Geoffrey consider himself lucky?
4. Why did Geoffrey challenge Will?
5. Will maintains he wasn't kidnapped – explain.
6. What is Will's plan for Lucy?
7. What is going to happen Will now?

Vocabulary

1. venomously 2. hypnotic 3. trance 4. invariably 5. arrogance 6. hermitage 7. complexion 8. reiterated 9. amicably 10. scowl 11. cavort

CHAPTER 21

1. How did Carrie's father show his pride?
2. The new school year brings new ideas – what were they?
3. What had happened to Zach's dad?

Vocabulary
1. blitzed 2. disfigured 3. dense

CHAPTER 22

1. How did Zach's death affect Will?
2. Why do you think Will wouldn't talk to Carrie about Zach?
3. What advice did Geoffrey give Will as he left?
4. How were the Little's considerate of Will's feelings?
5. What had Will never done in his life?
6. What did Will think of cycling?

Vocabulary

1. declensions 2. corrugated 3. divest 4. dispense 5. ornate 6. indolently 7. undaunted 8. incentive 9. hoar 10. transition 11. ebony 12. inanimate 13. dexterity 14. eke 15. sojourn 16. flamboyant 17. communal

CHAPTER 23

1. Where had the flowers gone?
2. How is Carrie's mother treating her?
3. Why wouldn't her mother let her wear shorts?
4. How was Carries going to get books past her mother?
5. What did Will think about toughness and weakness?

Vocabulary
1. darns 2. wispy 3. engrossed 4. vulnerable

Ingram Content Group UK Ltd.
Milton Keynes UK
UKHW021056280623
424178UK00020B/651